Sea Table

off the M6

Henri
Cenn

Kelvin Corcoran

Sea Table

Shearsman Books

First published in the United Kingdom in 2015 by
Shearsman Books
50 Westons Hill Drive
Emersons Green
BRISTOL
BS16 7DF

Shearsman Books Ltd Registered Office
30–31 St. James Place, Mangotsfield, Bristol BS16 9JB
(this address not for correspondence)

www.shearsman.com

ISBN 978-1-84861-421-5

ACKNOWLEDGEMENTS
Earlier versions of some of these poems have appeared in the following
publications with my thanks to their editors:
*Blackbox Manifold, Canto, English, The Fortnightly Review, Molly Bloom,
Painted, spoken, Zone*, and *The Arts of Peace*, an anthology edited by Peter
Robinson, 2014.

An earlier version of 'Words Through A Hole Where Once There Was A
Chimpanzee's Face' was published by Longbarrow Press in 2011 (thanks
to Brian Lewis). The first version of part 1 of 'Sea Table' was published by
itinerant press in 2012 (thanks to philip kuhn). An earlier version of the first
part of 'Glenn Gould and Everything' appeared in *The Writing Occurs As Song:
a Kelvin Corcoran Reader*, edited by Andy Brown, 2014.

Cover image by Madeleine Corcoran.

Contents

Words Through a Hole Where Once There Was a Chimpanzee's Face

GOING DOWN

Then I was falling and blind
and an angry man was roaring
in my face   and it was me.

The descent beckons
            as the ascent beckoned.
                        Memory is a kind
of accomplishment,

Oh Dr Williams you clever man
your words came to me in hell
to feed the insubstantial dead.

That's right over to me, come on Bill
it's alright, come on darling
I won't let you go.

Shall I roll you over in the clover?
we're nearly there now,
I won't let you go.

Melanie how on earth
did you carry us through that night?
I saw you walk the black river returning.

Book 11

And when I was down there
this was in my mind
even though I was not.

The unnumbered dead
the blurred and breathless dead
brides and young men and old men.

Massing for blood honey sweet
the nations of the dead and you
sifting through my hands – a shadow.

Lee has sent me a book – *The Wonder Book of Wonders*. On the cover a deep sea diver in a weighted suit sets to work with an acetylene torch, as fish swim by and submarine plants waver. There's an accompanying note, 'I found it in a second-hand bookshop in Harlech and immediately fell in love with the amazing cover. It's in fairly good condition, except on page 88 someone has cut out the face of the chimpanzee. Hmm.'

             wet season
                      most for
          animals earth
                    Herr Forelegs

I think I grew up in fear
my dad's alcoholic behaviour
unpredictable and cruel,
you never knew which way it would fall;
– well, it sharpened the wits
but wore out the heart.

                 *

And indeed the male chimpanzee
makes a family nest in a tree
and sleeps under the shelter on guard
he dreams of words through a hole.

                 *

In the darkening room Pat
– how come you make me talk Pat?
– I don't know, I really don't,
it just happens that way.

I was blind and suffered some short term memory loss because that area of the brain was hit by the blood clot. I was unconscious, then raving and had to be told what happened because I've no memory of it.

It's a trauma for the brain to handle, I know how it feels. I can see fine, with some colour confusion – bright reds and pinks drain to bronze – but with greater clarity, oddly, though the world is busy, intricate surfaces invading my eyes. Unexpected harsh sounds hurt and I see the noise.

Apparently I vomited copiously and kept shouting – help me, help me. I kicked out at the equipment around the bed. – You kicked out like a horse in a box. Apparently I would only do what Melanie said. I shouted – Tell that fucking man to stop fucking shouting. There was only me shouting, perfect. I babbled random numbers.

I saw faces floating over faces unseeing. Held out a hand to you, touching your nose and mouth, and said – This is your face isn't it? 4 a.m.

Brian emailed. – If you're well enough for me to make the journey. I will try to ensure my face doesn't assume a default setting of concern, although my face has but two default settings. You don't want to see the other one.

*

I like to think of Lee sitting at the window of his flat in Brighton, marine light making shallows of the high ceiling. He turns to page 88 in mild surprise at the absence of the chimpanzee's face. – oh.

*

Herr Forelegs waits at the door
a lurking confident bastard
his shirt of bloody platelets
his heart like a fist – bastard.

*

The greatest risk of another stroke is during the four weeks following the first. Two weeks to go. The ABCD2 model also suggests the odds are with me. Cold cold prose, clear as day. Come on you anti-coagulants – take these chains from my heart and set me free.

Sentenced to Wonder

An open air church in California.

The marvel of bird migration.

A lifting magnet empties a truck-load of iron scrap.

The Vatican is a wonderful city in itself.

Air is practically a non-conductor of electricity.

A temple of the Doric order in the heart of civilisation.

The helmet and chin strap are composed entirely of bees.

Pompeii was a sort of Roman Brighton.

The victor ends by tearing her opponent in pieces and eating most of
the body.

Many keen brains are at work on the problem.

A man in a weighted diving suit,
acetylene torch in hand makes wrecks fit to float.

The air's pumped in and she rises,
barnacled guns and Kitchener dancing a jig.

But see she floats grey and mighty,
big as a town, ready for salvage.

*

John Coltrane bends time
Bach straightens it out again;
stay with me boys
be at my side, my left and my right.

*

A recording of *The Text of Shelley's Death*.
Alan adds a note, – it might seem an odd gift,
but no, it's perfect.
To be avoided:
– romantic sailors
– romantic sailor poets
– death bed confessions
– sea bed confessions
– boats.

*

Ian's voice recognised
a back bearing shared
small town boys foot it
a blink in the world.

Herr Forelegs made his smell,
– Do you really mean to keep fighting this?
On the other side of seeing
in the crowded darkness, you belong to me.

I can wrinkle the world in front of your eyes
make the familiar unfamiliar,
spit you out like gristle
like a knuckle bone, like nothing.

September out this morning
taxied to the blood test
September at ease the sun risen
the town gets to work its logos.

*

Peter – just walked in to hear this
fell down a mountain, it was nothing really;
let's have no more from the fibrillation department,
it has pestered you quite enough.

*

John's voice on the phone
returned from Finland
the lakes and the land and the lakes
the breaded fish for delight.

*

philip called from the
dark and stormy moor
philip called a climate
of fathers to do me good

Herr Forelegs called
leaning in at the window,
– just checking on progress,
with eyes for inner darkness: the shit.

*

Geraldine emailed
Oh Mr. Headache
you poor little poppet
get proper better soon.

*

Andrew called, his voice
his restorative conversation,
here is your vision returned
you must come and see us.

*

Goldberg skips decorous sprightly
along the neural tracks,
down the digital wood dark and deep
light walks through the trees.

He stared at death. Death stared straight back.

These trees look designed,
them birds is on fire
in loops and swirls the sky ablaze.

A radar script inscribed,
What does it say? What docs it say?
The word as non-conductor of electricity.

MRI shows the riot here and here,
let it rip Elijah, roll us in your boat;
phosphor trails a migrant route.

*

And then later, after I returned, you told me,
when you were sitting there by the bed
and talking to me and talking to me.

You opened my eye, my left eye, carefully
fingers opening the lid and there was nothing,
nothing there, just a milky absence.

Melanie what were you thinking
when I was lying there blind?
Did you fear I could leave you so easily
or return a shade with nothing to say?

I didn't see any of this from above, from the ceiling,
but I would see you leaning over me, your dark hair,
your eyes stare down burning
like the first night we spent ourselves on each other.

Rain-soaked fields at rest in darkness,
owls and foxes rooting out fresh words;
hidden music sounding from the earth
at each risen station another world.

I would always want to touch you again,
to know what you are wearing, touch your face;
there's no shape for me out there if not you,
our days like turning light open in our hands.

katabasis song plays backwards

up from earth, random numbers

dry grass close unfocused

this last word last katabasis

AND COMING BACK

1.1

Three women walk down the street
red coat, black coat, something else coat
because it's Saturday in England in winter
their cortex clip-clop echoes all along.

I think their memories match what they see,
I think they draw their colours from the literal,
the bare tree photographed by grainy sunlight
as they walk into town without a folded map.

From the aerials of the assembled cars
there's no network of messages circling,
no lament rising up from the shiny river,
but on its surface everything's about to go.

And if it was today the sky failed, the year
turned a bed of darkness and more darkness,
under it all the learning of the world waited,
all the learning of the world, packed and ready.

1.2

Red pulse beating black along the line
like an arrow meaning I'll be there
to meet you and read the book of the living
and see the moon float on the dark river.

The chapter of coming forth by day;
the chapter of giving a man a mouth.
The chapter of giving a man a memory,
of not walking upside down in the underworld.

To see the full moon suspended over us,
an unknown yellow world, its practices
lettering the sky for delight of the mind,
to set free the heart lighter than a feather.

The chapter of the raising of the body,
of making the eyes to see, the ears to hear,
setting forth the head, of giving it its powers,
coming forth from yesterday, coming forth by day.

1.3

To walk away from all of that
and to say I know you, I know your names;
the mind making its own patterns
along a low horizon of muted light.

I think I taught that girl, worked with that man
but no, only in Apophenia, not in the world;
and then to walk away from the buried life,
the trees designed and the light contrived.

I know you, I know your names,
dark ones at the door, sharp ones at the gate,
shadow swallower, eaters of the thinking meat;
my legs hurt, tell me I'm coming through.

From here you turn left, then right at the lights,
the cars pass in a dance, a sports ground there
and here are the shops and the banks of the day,
as almost remembered on the other side.

1.4

Imagine these poems of the ordinary ascent,
blinking sightless at the cardinal points;
to make a series of journeys above ground,
to know the names holding up the sky.

Here the banks of lights, houses, circuitry
descending to the river as if stepping down,
and in the air above the idea of a river
the satellites call and the trees darken thought.

A man in a red t-shirt suspended above
in a square of yellow light conducts
the dancing mind in the field of offerings,
the hidden city assumes its shape and returns.

Let me follow my heart at its season of fire and night,
and in the days of seeing let me see;
a field of flags, a flight of birds,
the waters of the world in flood.

2.1

Eight Things About the Arctic

At 71 degrees north darkness crowds over the rim and from November to January the sun rises only in your mind.

We're off the ghost of Finnmark; to distinguish mountain from cloud from sea at this lassitude is unlikely.

In Honnigsvåg the faces of tourists rip and fly over the white hill above the town removed by the wind and set free.

Think of the miners of Kirkenes stepping down into a cold mouth as the price of nickel rises around the world; somewhat ferromagnetic, Old Nick underground takes a high polish.

The weather machine cranks out its orders where time zones meet at the crossroads; bury it and move on through fields of ice, forests of seeing.

Broken plate ice, one slab snow smooth decorated by the claws of a bird – pitter pat Mr Snipe.

Arctic convoys and U-boat shadows resurface; once there was a country called the Soviet Union of Uncle Joe.

If you pass the Lyngen Alps at night under a round, full moon the whole world is a dark photograph.

2.2

If I were looking for the source of chill in my bones
I might find it in Kirkenes harbour on the Northern Cape;
the abandoned Russian trawlers, a crane, white walkways,
leave me here where nothing moves.

We see the assembled gear and hidden lives,
lit from far below, silent and ready to play;
the King of the Arctic has quit to find the start of it all,
vacating a snow covered office chair on the dock.

And if I were looking for that cold cold answer,
in the last brilliant compartment of the sun,
the church bell would ring out its contours on the air
compressing the water to picture a polar sky.

Rolling out the sound condenses over ice,
sea smoke trails the boat, twists of light letter the air,
a language holding low around the edges of the world,
empty and endless for the mind to lodge at zero.

2.3

Another Eight Things About The Arctic

Ploughing into a headwind through the Barents Sea has turned this boat capricious.

Today Nansen you will study the sea running flush under the transparent shelves of vision.

The Sami say you should be quiet and not sing of the northern lights, be quiet and watch or they will come and kill you – but you can whistle them down to Earth.

You – pathfinder genius, limbs and head full of souls, lead us out on the thin skin of the unthought world, step by step to the oracles of snow; beat it out, beat it out and we'll follow.

Meteorite deposits called Satan fell to Earth to be buried here and rot your bones boys.

A cathedral sky breathing white and green waves and arcs; an electric pelt stroked by Chagall.

The King of the Arctic, his furs and people about him, has gone looking for the source of the chill in his bones.

Ptarmigan, snipe, seal – picture me dark night food; reindeer trot faster faster, sing it magical.

2.4

I saw Glenn Gould drag a piano to the North Pole
to find the perfection of number, the last of the land;
after the magnetic function of the Goldberg principle
and the hexagonal abundance of whiteness dancing.

And in the name of rhythmic continuity
and the abstract necessity of those structures,
I've taken my time to say these things to you;
the contrapuntal requires such deliberateness.

Looking back he saw the line of footprints
and knew another person not himself made them,
from this side of that other life survived
small red pools of light dotted the high latitudes.

Through the harvest of smoking ice, under a blue dome,
Glenn Gould took 32 steps northward into vision;
took fox sweep, dog bark, sparrow cheep
and the sun returning transcribed a new score.

3.1

With my ear pressed hard against the door
of the Thomaskirche I heard music,
voices through the locked door, a cantata
on the other side, deep in dark wood rising.

Picture in there a contrapuntal interior
of reformed air, stone and light flying,
for the architect of sound at play
up into the roof's incline of 63 degrees.

Dear Goldberg, do play me one of my variations;
da rump pa dump pa de is all we can say,
this music written for connoisseurs
for the refreshment of their spirits.

Da rump pa dump pa de, said the great transcriber;
the horizontal wind rolls up the European plain,
smacks the spire from the past into the future
to release a little aria dancing over Saxony.

3.2

Blue hills of Argos like distant smoke
drift into Arcadia and the fertile valley;
white on white, after such blindness
we sat in the courtyard of a Greek spring.

We sat in a box of no sides, the air moving,
to read *The Book of Things* by İlhan Berk,
saw the resinous pine tree – pefki
rise over the rooftop to net the names of the sky.

The mountain is a thing Taygetos,
the rusted showerhead speaks water,
the eucalyptus soft blond bow I cut,
the sea a question answered.

George, this might be a way to talk:
stones, ambergris, a fat bee awake;
against history the morning dance
and Souad Massi opens her mouth to sing.

3.3

I walked to the harbour for seeing
Yorgos made his boat ready,
a girl swam far out, way beyond the island
and the light filtered the rain with a message.

Facing death, love waits there in the deep,
as the lights burn out and the wires melt
the one word to bring to that moment,
the one thing to hold onto at the dark door.

Here in the month of fair sailing a soft wind
sifts the garden world of agalika and lavender,
two women talk in the afternoon, stop and talk;
listen to the rhythm underground, hands buried.

The air's a chamber of bird song and rain,
everything caught in the great rush of Spring;
that we're here at all in the dancing trees,
standing on the green entangled ground.

3.4

All night the storm stamped and blew,
wind offshore flattening the sea
running fast, suppressed and lethal
every leaf, stone and tile stands discrete.

The sky strums the wires all morning,
wear gloves for scorpions and snakes;
– Do you hear the singing underground?
No, only the white roots whisper.

I've had no news in weeks, nothing;
Leonidas, Augustus advance their sharp shuffle
but you'd best be ready for Alexander's sister,
How fares my brother? Oh he thrives, he thrives.

Yesterday a girl atop a white bull
went swimming past, Europa, the fool.
What sort of prospect is that?
Oh his sweet breath, his low moan.

4.1

Telemetry, telekinesis, Telemachus, holy shit.
Tell me another one, I thought him dead but he's back;
I thought him white bones cast on black sand,
his grin from the photo I inherit – and a world of trouble.

What zinger popped this one out, what fat mouth?
Radio Troy in the Greek Administration Zone:
father son reunion spells big trouble in Ithaka;
I might as well talk to the waves for sense.

But he's back, ready for action, ready for blood;
he sees himself in me, I'm far from fighting I said,
but then my heart fills – and this is the hard thing,
I've longed for him all my life.

He smells of smoke, drops into deep sea silence,
eyes wide, controls his face at sudden sounds.
What does it take to hollow out a man?
Black bones on white sand, his voyage, my voyage.

4.2

Of course he's come back, I knew he would;
they do go on the quality, like it matters:
pigs I understand – them I don't get at all,
but this one, not just crafty, he invented it.

They say the sea spat him out, he tasted tough,
spat him out in a river for a good wash.
They say a lot of things, there's a world of saying
and he's the best, it just tickles off his tongue.

He knows which side his mattress is buttered,
always has, my lord, that's why I like him.
I know I stink very bad, and I'm old but true,
it makes me young to look at him, like a boy.

I wonder if they'll sing their duet tonight,
banging her up against that bloody tree thing?
He'll get to it after the killing business,
a sort of cleaning up of screaming and smoke.

4.3

I didn't think he would ever return,
our lives apart unravelling, blue thread
floating on the air, a lost word gone pelagic,
but he's here, substantial, salty, like before.

His blank Trojan stare tells the story,
burning towers, lamentation turned to art;
I feared he was become no man nowhere,
and now it makes me hungry to look at him.

I was to be the woman surrounded by men,
the pack of them, soft, lascivious, grinning;
the light went out of me when he sailed off,
I poured my heart into a hole in the air.

Every night I talked and talked to an absence,
I've drawn him back, on and on I've said,
to the rise and fall of the sea – I won't have this,
come back, you must come back and speak to me.

4.4

Large as life Ithaka rolling under my feet,
I never thought I would get back here;
the sea never stops moving, the land now and then;
but here I am, I hold my nerve, I make it happen.

If there's an account to be given, no problem,
I'll say what I did and did not do – straight;
ships drawn up, burning towers, a woman,
if there's a pattern to this it's only visible now.

So that night I lay to sleep on the threshold,
thought of the undoing of these men, awoke
to the grinding of barley, knowledge in my bones,
the house flooded with light and the voices I know.

They stare like I've returned from the dead – well.
I look at my wife and it makes me hungry.
Dogs, see what you'll never have, never taste.
Sweet slaughter of limbs, wetness and her belly.

A Short History of Song Set to Music and Abandoned

Totteling State

I want a Wyatt I want a Wyatt
a Wyatt of my own, a whisper
in the bones Poetic, she sets foot
on the green path laughing.

Wyatt wanted a ticket
for the Petrarch sweet talk class,
he sang secrets stolen in Italie
for Inglish poetry beginning.

Planted country matters
smack in the fat porch of Henry's ear,
left Puttenham counting syllables,
for with such craft he was not caught.

Wyatt was pre-lute, short on honey,
slipped a knife into the padded heart,
a jest a jest or politic ploy;
this is the song of Thomas Wyatt

To sing the Psalms in Inglish
to dazzle sweet spikey Anne
to make a template fine
red and ripe his revolution unfinished.

*

*The Hard Heart Consort to play a sackbut riot, rip it up and start
again, softened only by recorders and bagpipes as night descends
on the river of song.*

Thomas Campion

Aswim at the source of the Thames
airy Campion cut his lute,
swanning to the capital, head high
for the season of learning song.

Each syllable slips downstream,
bound in sound free floating
for the abundance of invention
on the sunlight river gleaming.

Now winter nights enlarge
and I've given the day to Campion,
played chess across the chordophone
living in a song, Amaryllis let's say.

Kelvin, how can you live in a song?
My head's hidden in the sound box,
I think with my fingers, the words just come
and glide where Campion cut his lute.

*

*The music: sing I Care Not For These Ladies but not
necessarily in the countertenor voice.*

For the Defence

'…everyday language is a forgotten and therefore used-up poem, from which there hardly resounds a call any longer.'
Martin Heidegger

1

Good reder, the workes of diuers others
Italians and so, the Latine complete, well
so can we, our tong is able to make
Britaine's gayn in that kynde a device.

Of harts Spring love fruite to rage
small hony, much aloes and gall,
the earle of Surrey and depewitted Wyatt
doe proue Englishe eloquence.

From grene yeares stalkying the chamber
to delight the minde, speake now
abundance in the eares of the unlearned
and feed them from your hand.

Good reder for my defence these Psalmes
these Songs and Sonettes singing plain.

2

To move stony and beastly people
and walk in Apollo's garden
where poetry may be found
and the wheel of Spring turned.

To send an apology from Arcadia
where rivers run and birds acquire their names
you must clap your hands over terraced walls
and drive off the black and green snakes.

To measure how Alexander or Darius
strove to be cock of this world's dunghill
dance the anti-strophe unabashed
against their trifling trumpet victory.

At every turn contend abhorrence of the lyric
and let the blind old crowder sing.

3

Lyrick poets
ballad pleasure
to be sung
with the voice
reach for your
harpe your lute
your citheron
seek fauor
of faire ladies
and bemoan
their estate
that would be
Puttenham
in their place.

4

Protestant, iambic and triumphant
Spenser sank the Spanish armada,
dropped his classical anchor deep
and the waves came rolling bright.

So when Spenser sank the armada
his ninth line detonated the sea,
set men flying in the magnificent air
the bloody waves came rolling bright.

He planted empire's seed in Munster,
the rebel Tyrone dug it up again
despite the reign of Englishe words,
sweet earth's all turned to aesthetics.

What does it matter now? Everything and nothing.
A genius of acoustics, lived his life on a rising tide.

A Thesis on the Uses of the Voice

The vulnerability of the human voice
Handel said, Oh Cleopatra, that we perish
and it's a fucking shame.

A woman stands there in a red dress
her mouth moving beyond technique,
the vulnerability, few parts of the body

Can match it for beauty unmeasured,
a blessing pours forth out of nowhere.
And then, what to do with the face?

In the pauses of song, what to do with the mouth?
This can go on for days, there's no singing in darkness,
no life above life: work the means at hand to the end.

*

That the voice can turn brightness outward
despite all defeat, his voice was as the tuned spheres.
You might give me some music,
a shower of gold or a hail of pearls.

This is it, this is it, sang Neneh Cherry,
some sounds some burdens can release
answered Tjinder Singh – those sweet birds
launched from the stave into endless blue.

Shakespeare didn't know Neneh Cherry,
he knew Cleopatra, in duet and then solo,
he gave her the best poetry, her breath iambic;
she was Greek, learnt Egyptian of necessity.

He words me girls, he words me,
this chop-logic lawyer, this boy emperor;
Octavian was never known to sing,
he owned the world instead.

*

Spring Campaign Song

Orpheus was special from the start
neither village boy nor hired mouth
he made the language sound
across the wires of the world.

Small green meadow green
covered in April flowers
beside the track on Taygetos
speaks his one word to the sky.

Make nothing of this
but a platform of earth
dressed in one-time electricity
of camomile, iris and vetch.

Orpheus remember what is done
make nothing of it but
a credible and miraculous green
sing out the song simultaneous.

*

In this fashion the glitter of her language
washed up on the shore lacing the rocks
white silver then gold turning a song
entered the Indo-European core
bright bright a river running of many names.

Sing or else, Cleopatra said – beck, hop, luffed.

Sing or else, Cleopatra said, so he sang,
the intricate arrangement of larynx and tongue
the pressed vulnerability of a living voice
to lead us from the flat opera of the soundbox,
she looked into his face, it was the whole world.

*

*Tweet tweet the echo chamber air and turn the handle on a million bird
pianola. Blow through the papery holes, phpp, phpp splendid, the whole
world comes rolling in, the intervals of splendour. Far off let a chainsaw
rip it up to warm next winter with resin and sceptical fire. Campion,
Keats and Baby Jack to form a queue, humming and a-plucking on a lyre.*

Richmond Fontaine at St. Bonaventure's

If you're there when Willy Vlautin sings
I fucked up again standing at the mic,
a piano slowly steps through the way of it
he sings and *I barely know where I am.*

I think this is not a performance,
in the darkness of the club we're made still,
the piano steps through it, *just lost in this world;*
all distance is closed by a man singing.

Willy Vlautin lives in Portland, Oregon,
my friend knows his hairdresser there;
this song is taken from Thirteen Cities,
I recommend this music as a life saver.

You might like to research the origin of the band's name,
in such ways you can travel great distances and not perish.

*

*(The song is 'Lost in This World' from Thirteen Cities
by Richmond Fontaine on El Cortez Records.)*

Thomas Hardy

Thomas Hardy steamed up on a motorbike,
English poetry tucked in his knapsack;
he dismounted and stopped writing the novel,
fool poets thought he rode an iron horse.

He'd not come for the conference on the death of lyric,
but chasing a mortal song and sweet fiddle tune
out in the field for the licence deracination grants;
look away, it's unbearable, and if you don't, unbearable.

Hardy could have strangled most poets with one hand;
he left behind narrative in the service of the rural poor
and stacked boxes of shaped stones, as a mason would,
crafted from injustice and the resistant heart of stone.

*

Thomas Hardy on Tour

In 1887 Hardy walked a trail of singing dust,
viewed the graves of Shelley and Keats
and the skylark burials of Leghorn,
went away and wrote his poems of pilgrimage.

The muse spoke clearly to him that Spring;
she said – You made me up, I'm projected from thee.
Time was a fiction, past and present made one;
music said so, the flashing central sea said so.

That scene in the cemetery stayed with him,
his fellow countrymen loitering on his shoulder;
Genoese semaphore, the anatomy of light
and all the mortal birds of Rome agreed.

Ivor Gurney

'If only this fear would leave me I could dream of Crickley Hill.'
          De Profundis.

Tracing Gurney on bright tracks I saw England,
the Iron Age ramparts, GCHQ's inverted mosque,
what's left of Rome, a badger sett, the parish bounds;
dark waves of sound interrogate the coded sky,
Arabic strung up in loops like splattered pearls
binding lives in the secret wood mute and veiled.

Field-song of trefoil
field-song of flood
of stars in the ash tree
sing out Cold Slad sing out.

For nightshift duty lie me down on limestone grasses,
let earth and rooks rise in the blood a mighty tide,
from blue Septembered hills free the mind at last
away from trenches, berms and roadside elevations;
over the land made safe for darkness and all the boys
he sees a civilisation of lovely knowledge fit for song.

Field-song of trefoil
field-song of flood
of stars in the ash tree
sing out Cold Slad sing out.

Tracing Gurney on bright tracks I saw England,
the iron age ramparts, GCHQ's inverted mosque,
what's left of Rome, a badger sett, the parish bounds:
he marches off under moonlight, arms thrashing
through ridge and furrow like an inland sea,
speaks green syntax of Hawthorn, May and Willow.

Field-song of trefoil
field-song of flood
of stars in the ash tree
sing out Cold Slad sing out.

*

*Arrange Georgian huff puff backed by a muted brass band; the Hardy,
Housman, Thomas choir in the tradition of denial harmonises, playing
anger management assurance to the sound of settled England of never was
faintly faintly never was, let glimmering Butterworth well up, let Asian
Dub Foundation rip helter skelter into Fortress Europe and end with voice
crackle of 'all the birds of Oxfordshire and Gloucestershire' filling the air
with space and everything swallowed by the wind in the beech wood.*

Housman and Graham

I was walking the granite peninsula
beside the Housman Graham star-lit fences.

They sped by in a motor car on a jaunt,
heads inclined, dipped in dial light, eyes bright.

There was only one thing they could talk about;
how to construct the bare line without fuss,

A gleaming gantry to scale the darkness,
to see a compact landscape close around their feet.

The old car shot by, Graham retuning the radio,
half-heard song like a river running filled the lane.

*

*The music: at the foot of the stairs, with someone clumping about above,
descends from the top of the house in a clear tenor, a heartbroken ballad
from over the border.*

Experimental Poetry

Experimental poetry exists in the speech of the people
on the tongue of a first lacustrine morning
talking aloud of all that matters and then ceasing.

That experimental poetry has never changed is an archaeological fact,
its fault-line running back to prehistory vents wafty abstractions;
if you set out by laying the plan of a ballad anticipate trouble.

Experimental poetry is an unsound source of income and leads to the
          workhouse,
it is to be found everywhere and is for the good of others assembled;
better walk the Valley of Stones and expect your friend to remain sober.

Experimental poetry wants a mad mother and a vagrant sitting on a bench,
wants them speaking their language adapted to the purposes of poetic
          pleasure,
living with the birds and trees and the hidden pulse in the life of things.

Experimental poetry is written in the terms of a conversation no-one
          pursues,
its secret gaudiness snagged on a thorn shapes the dumb wind in a
          remote spot;
experimental poetry exists in the speech of the people.

The Romantic Tradition

Keats is out there chasing another vocal bird,
skimming leaves, mulch and the circuit of odes;
he trudges the dirty river burning his lungs and
rests on the green altar where everything's ritual.

The green altar stands for the Great Romantic Tradition,
covered in the fingerprints of eager boys and girls.

Fat magnet, capstan, favourite haunt and project
for the tuberculin, addicted and immune deficient,
for every demon daunted MacSweeney made free
by sad song misery sweetly rendered in Birdland.

The green altar stands etc

Lift the trap door in the grove at the last turn of the lane,
drop down through zero, under railways, canals, history;
the music plays backwards, the roots make Neolithic faces,
those people from the village step up together as one.

The green altar stands for the Great Romantic Tradition,
covered in the fingerprints of eager boys and girls.

*

Play it forward Jah Wobble style
unearth the muddy subterranean mix
add that chorus from Tosca the sound of
revolutionaries at the gates of the lovers' city
to strokes on the big guitar swoon ah
then break
blow a soprano sax through a megaphone
full throat from Shelley and the Many
flaunting heaven slam car doors on the edge

of night   the sinister tunes of Morrismen rising
their occult gestures in a bonehead chorus
Shelley jingle jangles lost childhood diminuendo.

That Poetry Best Not Written

1   Beware the poetic voice which wants to be your friend and any poet who makes the same claim on your attention.

2   The poetry best not written is artful prose rather than poetry with little regard to the ear or other formal considerations. Most of it could be set down as prose and you wouldn't know from listening to it.

3   Instead of an awareness of what poetry requires to be written there is a foregrounding of cleverly worked images with a self-caressing cuteness.

4   The imagery developed in this sort of structure is a type of luxury item making unfulfilled promises about itself; it's circumscribed by the logic of the snap, photographic moment of the given stripped down plot, undeveloped situations and figures – the imagery only serves that purpose, it's rendered safely bound up in that formal chain.

5   The structure normally reaches a predictable conclusion telling the reader something meaningful, sad, amusing, or tragic about the human condition; it pretends to have reached this conclusion as a discovery.

6   So, this digestible hybrid of formica lyric lite produces anaemic prose cum limping poetry and is delivered in a strangely flat, modulated manner which aspires to a sort of ordinariness – I'm like you underneath, believe me. (See 1)

7   I think I read it to see if I've missed something but its mighty emptiness, oddly, just induces claustrophobia.

*

There is no music for this, only
the noise of dust, reduction and deafness;
play it backwards, it's all the same,
some dull fudgy bass fingered by an idiot.

All the Poets

All the poets were in one room talking and not talking,
I was asleep trying to join one note of bird song to another;
it was impossible, it was that sort of thinking made obvious
and the blank days were far apart, months apart and gaping.

– Well, that's just fine, the over voice said to the assembled,
some people like to go out dancing, others like us we gotta work;
fine, it reminds me of the one literature and decades of expansion:
nothing makes poetry happen, and all the poets said me me me.

I heard the reshuffling of the nations on hidden cards,
it was murderous, the markets going ding dong on the border
and the embossed names gouging trends across mineral lands;
this part isn't complex, just a form of repetition to dull the wits.

Nothing makes poetry happen, not manifesto, drones or regret;
but for all the faithful ploughing of the hexameter field,
for all that learning made to serve a clotted tongue,
poetry's already there, beating the bounds of our rushing days.

Ghost House

There's a ghost in my house
the ghost of your memory poetry
or what I misremember each day
and over which I walk.

R Dean Taylor sang this to me
when I was a boy seeing the future,
I danced that Tamla riff iambic
smack off a sprung floor.

Afterthought will nominate
ghosts unevoked but present
as if the house is big enough
to admit the clamorous crowd.

There's a ghost in my house
poets whisper in the walls
the sad troupe at last a choir
in my house raising one voice.

*

*Repeat the ghostly big guitar riff, 1, 2, 3, 4,
all the way through.*

Elizabeth Bishop

Elizabeth Bishop leapt from the tender at Santos
danced across the snappy waves on sprightly toes
and swam the muddy tracks to Vigia.

In Petrópolis one night she listened to the ticking rain,
the wealth of insects eating through the walls;
rain come rain on my effulgent, flowing garden, come.

She collected animals and cared for them,
a big fish, an armadillo, a crab and various humans;
she had the sharp eye hungry for the brimming world.

Magnetic north, the taste of iron faded far away;
she found how the green country answered her,
a hummingbird in foliage offering precise dictation.

*

*The music is to arrive from the future, to be played with cold hands, a
lost samba dark and buried, drunk and discordant with insistent insect
accompaniment in the manner of a heart-broken love song.*

The Senior Choir

After the glory found on lyric stairways
a theory of craft labour took hold in Cambridge,
the Sunni triangle of old learning and new money
made London capital of foreign occupation,
though Milton would refine the franchise.

At some point for the locals it all tilts
relaxing into their novels and morality,
at one time choirs on the street saved the poor;
if songs set us free, we already have them all,
called conflict of interest in the history of the jig.

*

Tap out a muted canon on the White Stones *of Jeremy Prynne, every
moment, every note counts; the climate is entirely musical. Each city
emits a loyal note, play it for all you are worth, at each station the music
accumulates as you go forward. The tempo is to be anthropometric,
expansive and exact; brass crescendo to clear the sinuses and eyes. Make
the cadence rain down, without thinking about it; strike the final chord to
reveal a fresh place.*

When I First Got Geraldine

It was a reading in Sheffield
                          the song
swooping and running on
compassion to lift up a child
a witness   against unkindness
against the pompous and powerful
and the other works of men.

And Geraldine was singing
the small parts of words
to get under their skin
before the scheme took hold
and I got it – just, *bloody hell
you what,* all the rubbish
wiped off the words for kindness.

Another time she was on a ferry
with Kylie and Kylie had the hiccoughs
and was a murderer or murderee,
the poor little thing, and the M.V. Kindness
takes us all to the other side
with Geraldine and Alan, Kylie and Nick;
across the River Tagus in the Spring.

*

The Kylie Minogue Nick Cave duet Where The Wild Roses Grow *is on the
cd* Murder Ballads *but we were singing all together* Happy Birthday To
You *late into the steely night for the dancing trees in the garden and the
taxis coming and going.*

Peter Riley

I think the way to read poetry

Bars of light fell on the page
and delight returned,
out of those black shapes life poured
the spars of meaning, struts and arcs.

Screw up your brows and peer at the words

In the ordinary commerce of our speech
syntax breathing its first immaculate,
somewhere from the back of my head
I don't know what I'm saying, it's allowed.

In front of your face one by one

Here now this book of Peter's and his reading,
little book in this various world
make your way with truths unfurled,
with night-time voice of house and quiet.

Believe everything you hear for as long as you can

I think the poetry landed me here,
a line drawn out to the origin of song
placed an invisible lute in my hands,
knotted my fingers in the sounding strings.

*

And the music – play any song sung by Grigore Leşe, sung quietly at night from a neighbour's house.

Let's have the Roger, Sydney

This is a song about Roger Hilton
reading the Four Quartets to Sydney Graham,
which he did rather well,
the Atlantic knocking the cottage all over the moor.

And both men and Rose flew up to God
armed with the Eliot, a few drawings and a bottle,
three faces like full-stops staring out of the porthole
see the Earth far below and unfamiliar.

Ah well, we never thought to stand before you,
said the three of them. I know that, said the moth,
nothing's changed by your trip, you won't remember,
just get on with your work, that's all you have to do.

This is a song about the space poetry makes
in the mighty works of Hilton and Graham;
Eliot was never better read for entertainment
and time can be held as a watch from a friend.

*

*Begin with Britten's sea interlude Dawn
played on massed kazoos then crash it
shanty in the yellow tone and manner
of pub warmth flooding cold night pavements.
Make a great fluttering in the godly air
for men and women to sing the yeasty blues
fade into the theme tune of Fireball XL5
my heart would be a fireball Plato said.*

Little Song Don't Fade Away

From where song comes
she walks asway on light
running shapely down the street
at the next turn whether the lyric
voices a new awareness of self or
the needs and rituals of a community
from the autonomic nervy system.

She comes on tippy toes pushing up the
drums back brain ape heartbeat mix
the whole field a net of lights tracing
the question of poor Keats and others
sitting on a sparrow's wing
riding cheery into endless night is perhaps
only known to us in song if at all.

*

Sound the Anakrousis then direct a tinkling
of musical frost and running feet at dawn
to make the world new, then sound the Katastrophe.

Sappho

Sappho hit the water and rowed across the Aegean,
popped out like a cork at the pillars of Hercules;
at this distance each stroke a trochaic ripple
joined word to word on the manuscript of the sea.

The gritty sand of Lesbos scours the hands,
shoulders ache, head thickens, sight fails;
bite your tongue, recall the springs of Aphrodite,
pull Sappho pull over the liquid lexicon.

Her voice entered the western lyric
on the gleaming tide of the capital
like honey in the ear to soothe then madden;
honey, then gall, stroke by stroke said Sappho.

*

*Play the lyre low on the water mixolydian mode with tympanon
for pace, on and on, to be heard even at this distance.*

A Nightingale Improvises

Last night from the hollow between here
and the first hill climbing towards the mountain,
a nightingale poured out its plural song.

Rising like a quotation out of darkness,
out of the dense plot of trees for tender
the glittering sea as backwash and a bass frog.

The manifold song lifted out of nowhere,
the middle register recitative, the ornamental trill,
slow liquid slide notes and the unimaginable difference.

We walk our shadows along the white road,
the night is singing, out of nowhere, the sound
the night is singing, everything is given away.

end of an improvisation

Sam Bailey

Glenn Gould
and Everything

1

Along Commercial Street at homing time
he plays Byrd's Sixth Pavan and Galliard,
we're so inland my eyes change colour
from playing the piano since Year Zero.

At night the dead knock on the words,
place the fingers of your right hand
over the left to free the object in mind,
that ghost singing behind the music.

There are those voices which travel
on time by train from Berlin to Leipzig,
three birds at distance aligned.

That the world may be an orderly pleasure
the chart's littered with its symbols,
everything from one thing for delight.

*

Along Commercial Street at homing time,
the air sits a certain way in November light;
at the dance school door she said to her daughter
– Oh well you've remembered that then?

– Yes I did, it would be good, don't you think?
and the words hover as if on the air eternal;
above the grey circuit of the tilting world,
raise my flag here, unfurled with the turning leaves.

The music clattered down the stairs and out the door,
she released her mother's hand and stepped up to tap.

*

He plays Byrd's Sixth Pavan and Galliard
and the winter trees seem to move accordingly,
spare transparent leaves of unremembered green
propose a season of satellites and backlit thought.

There's nothing to see here, just the earth turning
through an interval sustained, though I think I hear
the king shall reign for ever and ever, sense soon
returns and Byrd's bass line like the world breathing.

Sunlight steps up from the floor at the window
and I see everything come in and begin again.

    *

We're so inland I think my eyes change colour
sea shanties go unrecorded in the local cults,
only the sky whispers maritime, cathedral blue
for the circling beasts over fields of mud.

After a low in the South West approaches
the country shrinks and the money migrates,
you can imagine the spineless tribe in charge,
telling lies about the poor and their care.

The weather is not a sign of the human condition
but attention to it is one way to let everything in.

    *

From Year Zero to play the piano
he sat on the chair his father made,
eyes level with the keys suspended
his hands like birds descending.

Guerrero's technique and the folding chair
hovering 14 inches off the ground, no brakes;
his hands rise and fall and run thinking
to climb the black and white ladder of sound.

*

At night the dead knock on the words,
they come in from the street and line up
with their black mouths open, they tap tap,
on the empty heart of the poetry of the world.

The struts and curves wear and break, case obscured
the breath leaks out of them across the table.

A dark inheritance, that tap tap, then nothing,
a voice about the house barely heard
the other side of the wall, at the next door,
all purpose fails in the senseless dust it stirs.

*

Glenn place the fingers of your right hand
over the fingers of the left, good, now, tap tap.
Can you feel the exact pressure required?
Tap tap: that clarity calibrates the singing world.

*

He sets out to work with object in mind,
the shadow ace in layers, slight at this hour;
one sound answers another in calm geometry
and the landscape's there, with or without us.

At this point Apollo takes flight again
and the idea of music invades the world.

It says what we think we have we don't have;
the thought of a voice singing behind the door
discloses at last the shape of it all,
before we spoke against the wordless surface.

*

Is that ghost singing behind the music?
A faint responder in the great profusion,
from Lake Simcoe across the whole world
humming the safe passage in deep ocean.

Subject to the advance of a cerebral embolism
cell by cell the brain closes, a raging fire
he knew and let go of knowing in one move,
walked across the room and opened the door.

The sky pours backwards in bloody darkness,
the living medium of all that music gone;
and if the hand is part of the mind
it rose up and stopped and he let go.

*

There are those voices which travel
along the airways above the street,
one to another making the marvel
out of the slow evolution of speech.

Who placed these words in my mouth?
What shall we eat when we get home?
Turn around three times, hold steady
and tune the truth to everything.

Open the door, a second door of light
lies on the steps we climb to the lit world.

*

By train from Berlin to Leipzig on time
sky and flat fields, the first green of Spring,
there must be a name for this exact colour
a stand of birch surrounds the shining water.

Through Südkreuz and Wittenberg
listening to Glenn Gould turn the crank
of Herr Bach's magical banjo;
how would he have travelled here?

Wig flapping bird-like on a horse,
aboard a coach or roaring in a sidecar?
The horse runs and the heart will not stop,
the music pours out miraculous.

*

Three birds at distance aligned
lifting in a south west sky
examine the quality of experience,
then two, then the light running.

Layered vision in place where late
the low grey curtain falls.

Contrapunctus the faithless choir,
sparrows blackbirds risk their arm,
flit the garden as the weather beats out
bare hymns for us men and women.

*

That the world may be an orderly pleasure
rendered so by the architect of sound
even the spaces and intervals charged.

Singing the Goldberg to the waking birds
Herr Bach and Glenn take their morning walk
arm in arm around the Thomaskirche.

In the moment of human invention
a language immaculate and unambiguous
fills the innocent streets of Leipzig.

*

The chart's littered with symbols,
an asset floated here, a sell-out there;
expect a low front from the west,
starry signs for a prince views a food bank.

There once was a mythology of weather
but meteorology ruined it,
let brute cause out of the bag of the sky
and we had to be taught humility again.

Schematic rain rains on the just and unjust alike
distributed unevenly, an unkind music in the air.

*

30th Street Studio Manhattan
Dear Mr Gould Dear Mr Davis
deep in the wood panel
resonance under a kind of
blue and Goldberg sky.

The child plays one note only
leans in to listen diminuendo
away from home a dark wood
the world a closing silence
and again one note, listen.

'Producing everything from one thing.'
In the heart of knowing, not knowing,
architectonic passing sound we are
music in the mind compresent;
everything from one thing, for delight.

2

Published for the Leipzig Christmas fair 1741
aria and diverse variations for the harpsichord
with two manuals, for forty Louis d'or,
from nowhere or Count Keyserlink's pocket.

An arrangement of sound held in the air
speaks the idea of a rational world, one voice
not one voice in that sort of dance, the mind
like music moving makes another space.

To walk by an elaborate colonnade
without resolution or climax, each step
substantiating a ground bass, each step
as if from nowhere on earth accomplished.

These pieces of a soft and lively character
symmetry in every part as if just found;
listen, here's someone cultivating good art
Bonae Artis Cultorem Habeas.

*

Bonae Artis Cultorem Habeas
arranged in variation 9 his signature sounds,
chromatic bar embedded in the fabric
B natural intones the secret art made known.

And yet for all this talk of counterpoint,
the mind as singing thing at first light,
what does it say as we walk off into the woods
knowing the thread runs out or will one day snap?

Count the knots as they slip through the fingers,
descending into the Thüringer Wald at night,
darker still the indifferent birds and beech stands
for the fables lost on hidden paths and buried.

Here in music coming and gone
caught in this scene and devices,
a voice says – do the work you must
by the means at hand to the end.

3

Up in the high room on the sprung floor
from their mothers' thin-lipped aspiration,
the young girls circle and dance – whump whump.

They walk long-legged in the street, through the door,
two boys slope by grinning, – ha, the old dance school,
delectation whets their eyes – whump whump.

Up there in the sky, dance girls dance, for all you're worth,
teeter on the starry blueprint above the town's design;
the piano threads a silver trail for you to set your foot – whump.

      *

      What little music they allow me here
      like dry bread crumbles granular,
      confined to nothing neurones firing blank
      just imagine the reverse, the opposite nowhere
      of the opening of Partita number 4
      so that absence ascends the empty air.

      Only background radiation wrapped in itself,
      imagine the arrowed shadow of black birds.
      What rooks? execrable spelt Stravinsky?
      darting over the canopy of lit trees
      what sycamores? Anyway that's it,
      shooting across the boundary of the world.

      *

Cathedral clouds coming in
we might fall from the land's end,
sky spinning the sea around
the compact fields telemetry.

Foxes running the dark fold,
the old dog-fox stares straight back
the cubs darting like sparks
on the edge of vision in falling light.

*

Hello, it's ok, ah, I was thinking
out of the Arctic night of radio waves,
What time? Does it matter? The earth turns
whiteness, you know about what I said.

To travel north, sun down for one season
and return to the latecomers, their stories,
spliced and reglued voices elide a climate,
at sea, a south west wind smack in the face.

If you return after long absence
you smell heather from the cape.

*

Walk across town and back content
to see the green plastic Buddha
a model of an inter-city train
a varnished guitar with no strings,
my eyes filming November sun.

I knew then the meaning of airflow,
circuits of action, oxygen absorption,
though the day was dark and down
all of us walking the ballad
de terre vint, enterre tourne.

*

Leaving the black hut I hear
the ice lake crack and chime,
the wind in the snow-heavy trees
answers in A-major I think.

What sort of trees? White shapes on white shapes.
Countless phrases dance glissando in the clearing.

I know it's impossible but remember
my mouth's stopped, my hands still
the doors frozen shut, a solid wall
the mind full of whiteness sounding.

*

One morning you catch the rot of leaves,
the layered problems of the poor, a lost estate
left hanging between the stripped trees;
nothing on earth recommends it.

Vapourised on the breath after the work's gone
the mineral stain leaches out for years,
walking in the shadow of the splashed negative,
there's only a memory of the colour of her hair.

There's only the self-effacing ideology,
down the narrow street the sky doesn't peel back
the walls close in like iron syntax,
half-heard that near music boxed as not for us.

*

I pored over maps of the region
Great Bear lake and Great Slave,
far north possessed of magnetic powers
one true note rolling underground
a wave synaesthesic and undiminished

Rises from bergs, sea, the blue and white land,
the voice a shape in air at these latitudes,
a halo of high altitude ice crystals
a mineral order acquiring a value unearthed
and the ghost talking low on the water.

*

Another day floating off on the big white bed
sky turns white and an unidentified bird sings,
monochromatic his analgesic song
rising to fall and spill from the edge of thought.

No other music joins, even words slip
send the whole enterprise on the tilt.

And here should be – one day at my window all alone
I saw the truth revealed but no, asleep what, 500 years?
The blue roofs at the back of town run on, bright
stepping stones, the sound of distant traffic enough.

*

I didn't like the piano, on the other side of it here,
my tactalia of the harpsichord in flight;
I remember attack and release, air flowing backwards,
my sense of the horizontal line rather than the vertical.

How can I tell you? I can trace the dark coast,
adrift but caught in a series of acoustical events
inside the sound of another human voice;
how close the mute restraint surrounding me.

And further along the passage, the mind
a garden emptying itself of song;
the dunnock, the nuthatch, the sparrow,
no attention can equal: all gone all gone.

*

Early morning ice cracks across the park,
we're privileged to wear dark coats and boots
to go shopping in the free market for essentials.

This is an allegorical picture called recovery,
a return to conditions that led here in the first place
and the one language won't do for the other.

There are facts and events or opinions and remarks,
weigh the portion of each presented, stamp on the ice;
it's not my opinion that the sky is blue and unbound.

The bare trees around the park look brown near black,
they won't turn green yet, so you see through the branches,
see the shiny cars zip along the roads in town.

*

I drove through New York in blinkers,
left a horse in a field of light ecstatic
capering tip-toe, bounding the scales of day;
try variation 1, try leaping the fence,
a rhythmic continuity as if just born.

I nailed my 32 theses to the church door
of the 30th street studio – tap tap done;
I remember the sarabande and street songs
ghosting the Goldberg in darkness,
an x-ray of the score and my hands thinking.

*

The miraculous music of the living
pours out of one mind to another to another
into the ears of how the mind is made,
wearing Bach's face, Glenn Gould's.

The unaccompanied singer fresh off the boat;
stepping through the world without metaphor
the miraculous music dances thought tip-toe,
the song escaping us all in or out of time.

*

As a boy he defended the fish of Lake Simcoe
roaring along the shore, the fishermen shouting.

After cold war tours to amaze the Muscovites,
recitals in Tel Aviv and Jerusalem of early Israel.

With all Bach recorded to begin a variation
on the Goldberg Variations, to make it new.

Enough, it's enough, hands up, step back to the lake,
he's rattling the old Chickering serenading the birds.

*

Up in the high room poised on the sprung floor
you shoot across the boundary of the world,
stand on the edge of vision in falling light
smell the heather out at sea from the cape.

The ballad of *de terre vint enterre tourne;*
the mind full of whiteness takes soundings,
half-heard that near music boxed as not for us.

The ghost goes talking low on the water,
stepping-stones, the call of distant traffic enough
no attention can equal, all gone all gone;
see the shiny cars zip along the roads in town,

An x-ray of the score and my hands thinking
the song escapes us all in or out of time,
rattling the old Chickering, serenading the birds.

Sea Table

1

From this wooden ramp
the total blue spectrum
lifts the sky westward,
the wave cache ascatter

Shaping the Neolithic deal
and Mycenaean rethink,
my table at the window
sets off into the gulf.

John Gould owned this table,
then David and Linda;
he drilled eloquent into the past
we all crowd around it.

One leg tilts, a saucepan ring
embellished in soft pine,
cast off into white particles
launched from the slipway.

       *

Change came hand to hand
along new exchange routes
dreaming a map of desire
goods and beliefs unwrapped.

Copper tin gold silver
amber marble lapis lazuli
oils perfumes wines we want
trained horses and wives.

Change came across the sea
on a boat, men with different hair
their words on the water
their eyes sea-green asking.

How do I get over the shape
of your mouth its upward
promise eyes wide around
the words into which I fall?

*

Orion rises over my gate
rests his right foot on the tower
there's movement in the sea tonight
but no fireflies flicker in the harbour
no thoughts ignite the world.

Only the lit graves of Easter
keep the dead with us don't
let them go into the falling darkness
that's your own life you see memory
a stream of cold air in the riverbed.

*

Renegade, excommunicant
Platonist, revolutionary,
inventor of the Renaissance
beloved of the Medici.

Gemistos / Plethon
opens his pagan box,
draws up to my table
and looks at the sea.

Here's the point Gemistos:
to set things right in their kind
is not a trick, secret law or CDO;
the end is different.

He walked the shore scheming
saw heretics flung in the glassy sea,
arms and legs broken – swim, swim;
true faith gasped at every breath.

From the lookout point,
the plain rolls out to Sparta
the future at his back westward,
further even than Rome.

The ocean of thy goodness,
thy boundless mercy to man;
the flow of ideas turns
and is fatal, yes we have no.

        *

Recordings of the sea from
several locations in Messenia,
from behind the tower
in bright April swimming.

In the harbour at night
wind and waves funnel music
the dark sea
working on its language.

Shingle channels in from the left
echoes an orderly sentence,
though the bay, the stones chorus
sounds submerged boustrophedon.

And a bird a finch I think
above the path back from the sea
lyric rising and falling
Spring visiting the world

On wings of digital mimesis
the god of the air releases
modulated below the red zone
his new ancient song with a bullet.

*

Mystras might rise and fall
the Ottoman tide turn but shit
my foot is riddled with something.

The fingers on my right hand
white and cold at the tips but
still there's an argument to make.

And another winter comes sluicing
through the Monemvasia gate to wash
away Aristotle and repaint the gods.

All night I dreamt I heard the sea,
the voice of the sea
in the blue morning made visible.

What is the light doing to the layered
slopes of the mountain and the cypress
climbing out of the dark folds?

Something without name
calls – Byzantium Byzantium
by morning visible for miles on miles.

Plethon meaning plenty, abundant
a furnace lit in Anatolia, Plethon pitched
between Sparta and a piss-yellow dawn.

Malatesta retrieved his bones
carted off to adorn Rimini and
invent the west's Renaissance.

Ships sink and without trade – nothing;
without the border guards' songs – nothing:
calculate the fallout of the Fourth Crusade.

*

A poor man runs by the table,
his hand takes the food, the light
shines through him, oracular.

The throne of dread necessity
occupied, the voice of fire speaks
in every square where reason lost.

Antiquities taken to order, clay figures
lamps, vases, a Mycenaean seal ring
a horse long-legged spare and free.

The running man loose limbed
running the force field bronze,
the light shines through him.

Boss, help me boss   iPad
see is good   stolen good
not Mafia look in the box.

Look I give you both help me
my family both €250 for my family
look I give you you take home.

In Monistraki, the desperate
a man in a suit of Ikea bags
woven blue underwater shuffle.

The running man flickers by
the newly immiserated
in procession under the Parthenon.

*

Radio Byblos on air
sang the Anne Carson summer
Big Money fails to buy
alphabet soup for the poor.

The starting point is
ordinary language and this
a claim from Gemistos
yes we have no bananas.

The water is deep
and we can drown
by repute it's crowded
all us men and women.

So all that summer
my neighbours were
the hummingbird moth
and the carpenter bee.

Boats out of the water
the empty harbour receives
bougainvillea wedding
and everything that is.

Swirling through Taygetos
light's gone behind the sky
we cut the eucalyptus, the pine
tuned the wind for winter.

Last square of sunlight
warmed my feet, a day
won from the season
the sea loading its gun.

So all that summer
my neighbours were
the hummingbird moth
and the carpenter bee.

*

Then set said table to breakers
four legs up, rigged a sail, held on,
paddled like mad, farewell
Koroni, Methoni, golden Venice.

There were days of no wind,
bands of darker blue proved false;
days under a magnifying glass
held every sound where it began.

Set course for the Cape
a periplus of the mouth of hell,
What dance is that? Against time
wave after wave, into the Aegean.

White engine of thought
brought to the table;
of marble, of obsidian
the first figures stand.

2

We found twenty signs on the way
though our boat was lost mounting that wave
and below us a ghost boat unmanned,
the water coiled black an episode in our mouths.

The terms, a wall of water running, slick clauses
of something we barely saw through;
we sang from boat to boat in darkness
– Are you there in the deep? Are you there?

We found twenty stones the way we went
by the way a language, not a language,
baked clay or composite, stubborn, gouged,
scratched out on the deck, chip chipped.

So we set an approximate course,
surrounded by the material principle
wave on wave for explanation;
in sight of land with people like us but not.

The stones speak where fathers hide;
at first after the wars, then from their children,
all the fathers in that sad place underground
where the sea sounds zero zero zero.

*

To rescue the drowning is hard;
some with arms raised, others O mouth shout
– How many of us can you hold in mind?
and some swim the graphite sea.

I don't remember the town I left,
only the sun filling the pocket of garden;
I remember that girl, her hair, full of light,
and walking all night to see her again.

A formal rhythm marks white blue white
assumes forward motion, the mind conspires,
each wave different but the same sea running,
all thought held in that furious pause.

There are no ladders under the sea's surface
though speculation wants it so, no step is taken;
though hexameters roll on, not a line will save you,
the dead drift like thoughts cast back in the mind.

There was an island where fresh water ran
my love would call from that greeny shore,
she filled my hands and lifted my heart
but she sang in underwater words to me.

*

We'd drawn up the ships and were waiting,
pitched the goods and talked our business;
had an easy sailing of it to these Greeks,
a tidy harbour, tucked away, wealthy.

Days went and the wind turned favourable;
a crowd of women and girls came down
sauntering in the shade of the stern,
they spoke their words, looked and touched.

Dib-dabbed their feet in wet pebbles like jewels.
What do you want? Look what we've got here.
Dib dabbing splashes, legs rising and falling;
then everything cracked apart in a single rush.

Everyone saw it in the same white moment;
some of them weighed next to nothing,
a half sack of corn slung over the shoulder
or a live goat kid say, hardly kicking at all.

Waves yielded, opening and closing like oil,
our transit of V and the plural ocean – stop;
that was our entertainment each night,
like dragging a fingertip through spilt oil.

*

I learnt their language letter by letter
reading the names of their boats;
Captain Adonis, Maria Sunday, Lifeboat:
the sea's glossary made me its drudge.

I also learnt to play the zither and the harp
to fancy up silence for common show,
I took up shop keeping and soft clothes;
I walked away from that, it had no flavour.

When rumours of Harpagus or another
closed like arms of a press, like jaws,
I ran to the west on the great slide of the sea
scaring the waves to find the unknown.

Voices of the village square remained,
an echo chamber Spring, of voices overlaid;
as the light enters a shuttered room
the first stories of the old – you remember when…

That island there, the soft blue curve of shore,
looks close, looks reachable and inviting,
but even with a good wind it's a hard days sail
and we don't know what trade they want.

*

And there I listened to the sea
the waves like grease in a pot
slip and slide from the spent storm
no bearing true, no surface sure.

The sea is a different place,
we tie and untie its chords all night;
what we know doesn't count
a song of the mind not in the mouth.

Do you think for all your artful calling
it will unlock itself and let you live there?
Just one day? See that block of basalt black?
Think of darkness, original night unyielding.

And we came to their empire afraid
made our way ashore to hidden villages;
it all began in a house underground,
inside a mound of dirt, a pile of bones.

Like a song in the mouth but not of the mind,
we saw signs that looked like pictures
snakes, birds of prey, four-legged animals
insects, abstract symbols, flat red stones.

*

Whether this was a plan of their harbour
or the altar of the unknown woman I don't know;
in the village there was no evidence of luxury,
they lived off shellfish, dolphin flesh, a little grain;
it was a centre displaced, lost to the new kings.

So we landed there, crunched up the white beach,
there was no business, the obsidian rush redundant,
there were no answers in the high places,
just the archipelago displayed like the first chart;
dawn drew her fingers across the face of heaven.

They had piles of figures in house and grave,
mostly female, their meaning forgotten,
their purpose for living or dead we never knew
but see how the tiny beauty fits in your hand
her limbs and breasts and tender V.

It was a warm still day, the air lucid at rest,
all thought suspended, not even the sea sounding;
there was no saying if you saw or touched it,
a substance drew you out and made you hungry,
it looked like the whole world laid out before us.

*

Setting out, the boat's heavy, low,
pots of oil, wine, furs and wax;
take the safe passage, nothing flash;
unloading our goods and stories
we ride off higher, just born.

These pots we use for ballast
empty of the good oil, the wine,
they go mad for them out there
those barbarians of the far west,
pretty up their houses, unbelievable.

So we Greeks went down to our ships,
not that abducting women meant much,
no more than any other plunder –
honeyed wine, shiny trinkets, decent meat;
we went down to our ships meaning business.

At first you see the sea lanes, the promise,
remember the markets, their special deals,
the girls and their ways; then it's battle lines,
then spar wreckage littering the shore,
Darius or another rewriting the terms.

*

Then without warning we came to
the god/morphine morphine/god moment;
the golden sun falling into those arms
the world turned music in every part.

And she, little Miss Poppyhead, took us
a-sing-songing to the hidden places,
the watered groves and coves the locals know,
the high meadows and the lookout point.

We came off the sea in rags, standing there,
a mighty thing at rest breathing in our faces
held us in silence, the sun leaning down,
in red wavelength red with water for bones.

She gave us honey that blonde, her bearing,
alert, inclined, I think herbs are involved
and bees on the hillside disputing their labour;
she gave us honey and spoke the dark word.

We left under a sky of layered pink,
might as well say we made up the dithyramb
saddled a dolphin like buckos
and rode around the mouth of hell.

                    *

When the world came crashing in
there was an eclipse, a day of flying fish,
the earth breathing, a night of vision
making the harbour a bowl of light,
then black ships to the end of seeing.

There was a Phocaea we always leave,
always a Massalia of arrival;
along the red routes for the next ore,
shaping a script like a lethal poetry,
finger tips white, then blood returning.

When news of Marathon reached Darius
he knew fury – he sent out messages
for ships and supplies to towns and cities;
he turned Asia upside down
to be shot of these Greeks.

So when the world came crashing in
we set our minds on a darker course,
saw empty spaces around the table
a lookout bird became a white rock
the light rippling red on the water.

*

Into the cave mouth, a wet hole in the earth
where it all goes, the end in darkness bidden;
not at the sea gates in blue light running,
not even a ghost of the bow wave whisper;
the sleeping stone cast and never retrieved.

We suffered the vision of closest things
the whole world washing around us;
thalassocratia drowned to support bees,
to house the pretty sea slug, the lichen spirals,
the crab waiting to loosen your sinews.

A fouled hull scours the soft flesh
the face, the genitals and suchlike,
the water's red but no memory lingers,
your dangling feet, dancing dancing,
below an unfixed blue ellipse closes.

No number. No glyph. No account.
Virgin Face. Bright Voice. White One.
Undone by half human song, made mad,
driven down into a ditch of no season.
Virgin Face. Bright Voice. White One.

3

My neighbour's music sounds across the square,
the song overwrought, claustrophobic, plaintive;
clouds of dust invade the house to settle in layers.

The fisherman walks by the tower and waves,
Nancy, Nancy – Yorgos, where is he Nancy?
Look at this, look, what happens next, tell me?

– Our ridiculous government, those idiots in Athens.

Words rise like birds driven off shore
scattered over the dark economy rolling in,
a country pirated, an evident blue removed.

4

Of course after all that there's nothing left,
grounded and scattered in the wet wreckage
born with a memory of the end in darkness buried,
driven down the magnetic hole, epistulae ex Ponto.

I've landed here, head bouncing on the messy table,
bright signals from everywhere burn my face;
there's only one action, one principle to follow,
radio waves flood the upper air calling and calling.

By day I live above the One Gate, look east for news,
abandoned on this shore in the marram and sweet vipers;
I've turned the poetry inside out on a rusty banjo,
cranking up metaphors with their roots exposed.

The city bright gleaming stands and sinks,
the smoke of riot clears and the poor are poorer still;
no man a house of good stone nor a painted paradise,
τραπέζι τράπεζα try eating what's spread on that counter.

Work out the big names, Xerxes, Caesar, Goldman Sachs;
who can translate this lot for you, trace the etymology?
But the music in the air at night is real classical, the song
flowing backwards as it proceeds – and it's not made up.

*

For Eleni's baby at the taverna it's year zero,
imagine the life that sparks and fizzes in his mind;
we come in from the night and revere him in silence.
Dimitrios – may the light shine on him strong as his grip;
Dimitri – may it go well with you in the crashing storm.

What you're hearing passes for news in the sliding world,
clowns play the numbers, bounce the market oopa oopa
and tax the air for breathing in a fire sale for strangers;

let the sea roar and the wind bend the trees unreasonable,
the halo around your perfect waking face holds still.

Even as the TV screen flickers over the pit, all's well;
you'll not be abandoned on the hillside or the sea's margin,
those irrational, brutal practices we no longer follow;
no child, no generation is sacrificed to save the powerful;
we stand in a circle around you to tell you this.

Here's Eleni's baby, his hands reach out to everything,
his eyes track every move and his face lights up the world;
tomorrow we fly kites for Clean Monday, the green the red,
we'll go out with Archylus and discover aerodynamics,
the green, the red, the dancing, and send our messages up.

*

On the TV screen heads shout in stacked boxes,
the killer word – troika troika and a country shrinks;
and my waitress is doing her homework in silence,
intent as the ground disappears beneath her feet.

She is Greek blonde this girl, lifting her hair
to show a neck white enough for a swan to grasp,
her wide apart eyes flicker Europa departing;
thunder rolls in the gulf, booming off Taygetos.

I am researching Amelia Earhart, she was a pilot,
yes, ah, that word, a vi a trix I am learning it,
what she did when she was alive, no woman did;
I am learning English and German after school.

The village boys saunter by her table, look away,
swim in the light of her white waterfall;
– It is my ambition, I would like to be a pilot,
to fly the crowded waters of the Sea of Abduction.

Outside the yellow taverna the world turns to night,
hauling in the silver lines of flight the sky empties;
the black sea calls to the land people, come come
the sea calls, calibrates the heart and spits us out.

*

Saidona was once known as little Moscow,
staring down in mid-air to an opalescent sea;
this is the buzzing spring of greening trees
excited and wired birds swoop and call,
spreading flowers rise high into the mountain.

Saidona is quiet, far off a man hammers his roof,
the aconite, anemones and spilling daisies
dance at the base of the memorial's white wall,
an account, the many names, the lines by Ritsos;
and the sky opens endlessly to the whole world.

In Saidona stones speak where fathers hide,
at first from the wars, then from their children;
Eleas Noeas survived the death camp in Essen,
returned home to be executed in the civil war
and the doors open as if nothing happened here.

Ritsos was exiled and imprisoned on Lemnos,
Makronisos, Ayios Efstratios, Yiaros, Leros, Samos;
he thought wrongly, wrote wrongly and survived;
his voice sings out from Saidona, sings out from stone,
sings out in the vertigo of Spring on a perfect day.

*

Scent of orange blossom floods the ruins,
stones taken from the plain for the city;
what's left of Sparta to raise Mystras
a final stand to fall against the Ottoman.

In the cathedral of Agios Dimitrios
the marble slab beneath the dome
bears the Palaiologoi double-headed eagle,
talons extended to attack east and west.

Constantine stood there to be crowned,
last Byzantine emperor, boss of new Rome;
looking up he saw the great Pantocrator glare,
the roundabout of prophets spin over Sparta.

The small cathedral articulates a message,
flutings form knots, animals jump and hide;
Plethon grins and capers from the prothesis
a centaur in relief after popular conception.

In 1464 Malatesta turned up all a-glitter,
took the lower town from the Turk
scooped up Plethon's bones for veneration
enshrined them in a hole in the wall Rimini.

*

The Paliatzis ο παλιατζής The Used-Things Man

Most days of summer from the white furnace
the used-things man calls – ο παλιατζής ο παλιατζής
broken fridges, bikes, chairs, water tanks piled up;
village to village around Taygetos.

ο παλιατζής ο παλιατζής coming in closer,
bring out your junk, I can use it;
his face is dark wood, subtle,
he's made of sinew and dust.

Psychopomp in a wrecked Toyota,
the air has eaten holes in its wings;
his woman doesn't move, her eyes flicker,
she sits by him, draped, fluid, watching.

ο παλιατζής ο παλιατζής – give me your junk
bring out your bosses, banks, economics,
your big ideas – you can keep the politicians;
see everything disappear in waves of heat.

He looks at what's left of a stripped car,
an engine block in yellow weeds;
he looks, weighs it up and drives off
pursuing better junk in the next village.

*

The road surface cracks after one summer,
a winter rain sluices down the mountain
takes its course and digs a trench
under the tower's slow turning shadow.

A black ship went by out there, close to shore,
dumbfounded men and a fat dolphin aboard;
we saw them, under full sail out of their minds
off Cape Tainaron and its good grazing.

The music on the water floated by,
we all heard their singing as one voice,
honeyed notes swam below the surface
the shining sea made calm to the edge.

From first annihilation to pressing word
they sang the song every turning hour;
interpretation would require a ritual,
an oracle, a whole troupe of exegetes.

They sat there, the wind drove them on
sailing back to morning, an unknown harbour,
their hands empty and idle, dispossessed
out of a clear sky: that was Apollo.

*

Bring to the table the glassy waters crash
the last run black bull in a wheel turning,
the war the poor will lose, the falling house
and the kingfisher zooming the harbour.

Bring animal heads set aside and grinning,
the withdrawal of international finance
and system collapse as a theory untested,
the first ear of wheat on a marble dish.

Bring to the table ghosted everywhere
a whisper imprinted on the chambered earth,
the empire of dust become an order of song
to salve the glamour burning our eyes.

Bring the vacant places the young abandon,
the light on the underside of wings leaving,
the dark window, the empty chair, the lost child,
the unimaginable mountains and sea untold.

Bring from the bloody ditch Ritsos the ghost
alive outside the bank in blue and white tatters,
bring the creatures from the passage underground
blinking in the light of common day restored.

                    *

Big morning steps down the mountain,
seeds cloud the air almost a substance
scattered everywhere to see atomised
Apollo of more than 130 names.

Over the sea's static and blue horizon
a litter of language laced the rocks,
bright silver then gold, a song rising
out of the meander of rubble and words.

To see the day lifting from darkness,
from the shadowed houses lives come
work the grain of the wood, the green wave,
a door handle made to fit the human hand.

Do you make music of the air kinetic,
send migrating light from afar,
tune your bees and release your birds,
set olive trees flashing high in the mountain?

They said if he paraded in the village square,
his attendants making shapes like thought;
he would change us, burning our shabby lives,
no-one would go about normal business after that.

*

Come sea wash lucent
over grainy wood wordless
wipe clean the slate
salt rot the stave
stain the cheap pine
sliding buoyant to
the unexplored shore
raise the ships of Oitylo
Ibrahim Pasha's fleet
the Don Juan the Spider
the bonny barque Ino
unpack our ignorance
in a deep bowl oblivion
over my knees knocking
over my frozen heart
drench my head
pour water words
O O into my mouth
talking and not talking
come sea wash lucent.

5

From this wooden ramp today
the sea like blue steel shines
a line of light on the edge of
day breaking on the harbour in 3D.

Water falling drawn into
a temporary white noise
song of the pebbles piling up
in every room of the house.

Make a mosaic of the air,
walk the stubborn tracks
the white stones, the leaf labyrinth
the light-invaded trees breathing.

Lady of the Way, Hodegetria
the inner knowledge
                              and the outer
show us the way   restore the city.

Today we have no petrol,
tomorrow we waste a crop of peaches;
roads blocked, post office gone, today
we have no times around the corner.

And then my neighbour called Helen
called, to speak about the troubles;
and it was a Greek morning for talk
and the history was hardly random.

            *

Waves break along the shore
packing crates, moulded polystyrene,
a red cap without a head.
Haul up.

Off that cape the deepest water,
invisible forest of blind depth
of bioluminescent forms.
Haul up.

Where Europa rides half sublime,
open-eyed with her darling bull
sparking little gods and goddesses.
Haul up.

Egyptians and the boys of
fifty towns, float open-mouthed
under a glassy shine.
Haul up.

      *

Late in the year a second spring
the daisies and the mallow
that patch by the chicken coop
making a show of nothing gaudy.

All we need, tender song
a fortune at the window, there
across the way my neighbour
sees his garden dancing.

Abjure dread necessity,
occupied by beasts:
that light a beginning
the voice of the fire.

Boats out of the harbour
the sea rolls in a dark season,
wind from the south, 7 to 8
sea grey, sky a lifting distance.

House tidied for winter
papers squared away, table empty
for another, Yasmina clouds
the courtyard, perfumes every room.

Last night we noticed the children
everywhere, as Peter said of Bukovina,
on bikes racing, jumping the harbour wall
in *kafaneio* light, they flit door to door.

All over the place, the children
tip-toeing next to rolling darkness
spray flying crowns them, everywhere
look – it's you, it's you, it's you.

Notes

Words Through a Hole Where Once There Was a Chimpanzee's Face

For the opening poem see William Carlos Williams, 'The Descent'.

'He stared at death. Death stared straight back.' See John Berryman's *The Dream Songs* number 45, 'He stared at ruin. Ruin stared straight back.'

A Short History of Song Set to Music and Abandoned

'Thomas Hardy On Tour.' See Hardy's 'Poems of Pilgrimage.'

'All the Poets.' The italicised line is from Lou Reed's 'Sweet Jane.'

Peter Riley's poem 'How To Read Poetry' is in *XIV PIECES*. Longbarrow Press, 2012.

The music for the final poem is a transcription of the end of an improvisation played by pianist Sam Bailey before a reading by Kelvin Corcoran on 9th February 2012 at the Free Range series of music, film and poetry events in Canterbury, Kent, UK. A recording of the performance can be found here, the section of the music that has been transcribed can be heard from 11.30 on the recording.

http://soundcloud.com/free-range/piano-set-9th-feb-2012

Glenn Gould and Everything

There is an account of Alberto Guerrero's teaching technique of tapping in *Wondrous Strange: The Life and Art of Glenn Gould* by Kevin Bazzana, 2004.

'Producing everything from one thing.' Schoenberg on Bach.

SEA TABLE

Parts 2 and 4 of the poem loosely allude to a ceramic of twenty small engraved tiles in a frame by Robert Wilcox. In part 4 the reference is increasingly allusive and abstract. See http://www.stivesonlineshop.co.uk/bob_wilcox.htm

The first poem in part 4, 'With usura hath no man a house of good stone', see Pound's Canto XLV.

The fourth poem in part 4. In Saidona, Messenia, the memorial for the Second World War and the Greek civil war carries an inscription from the poem 'Greekness' by Yannis Ritsos. Thank you to Maria Pavlidou, Yannis Voulimeneas and Lorna McFarland for their patient help in translating those lines and also for helping me find out what happened in the village.

> For years besieged from land and sea
> everyone is hungry, everyone killed but no-one dies,
> from the high lookout their eyes burn
> the big flag and the deep-red fire,
> and every dawn from their hands a thousand doves
> fly out to the four doors of the horizon.

Lightning Source UK Ltd.
Milton Keynes UK
UKOW04f2335130315

247861UK00002B/25/P